A Survivor's Guide

to

Emergency Preparedness

*How to Prepare for
Hurricanes, Power Outages,
Nor'easters, and Other
Storm-related Emergencies*

Rosemary Augustine

A Survivor's Guide to Emergency Preparedness

How to Prepare for Hurricanes, Power Outages, Nor'easters, and Other Storm-related Emergencies.

By Rosemary Augustine

Photographs and Graphics - photos were taken by the author; graphics were provided by *openclipart.org* and *memes.com*.

Cover photo is the author's own art work illustrating her interpretation of Hurricane Irma's fury over Florida.

Twitter posts and videos mentioned in the book and posted during Hurricane Irma can be found at: *Twitter.com/ZiggysSecrets*

Published by:
Blue Spruce Publishing Company
2175 Golf Isle Drive
Melbourne, FL 32935
Info@BlueSprucePublishing.com

ISBN: 978-1-943581-08-5

A Word From the Author

What constitutes a storm emergency? It can be anything that threatens your life, your property, your state of mind, and even your soul. How you prepare for a storm emergency no matter what storm comes your way determines how you survive.

As I look back throughout my life, I was four years old when I experienced my first hurricane. Throughout the years I have endured earthquakes, tornadoes, winter storms with power outages for days, not to mention many nor'easters, tropical storms, and, of course, numerous hurricanes.

This book is written to provide the reader with a list of items to prepare in case of weather-related emergencies, potential evacuation for hurricanes, or storm-related disasters. Preparing for any emergency, these lists are everyday items that should be staples already found in your home.

I have been through many storms some with power outages for days. I've lived in states where nor'easters were common and tropical storms were frequent. I have prepared with water and food for at least a week to 10 days, and have never been without electricity for more than five days. However, those days without electricity were even more challenging to me than during Hurricane Irma.

I learned my lesson years ago to be prepared - always be prepared. And, it never hurts to be over-prepared, since in the end, if you don't prepare for any storm emergency, you'll panic, make bad choices, and possibly lose your life.

I was never a Girl Scout. However, I've gone camping many times but hated being in the dark. You might even say that I'm afraid of the dark. Yet during a power outage, I'm fascinated by the serenity of candles lighting a room that was in pitch darkness. When I lived in colder climates and endured many power outages in the dead of winter, the combination of several oil lamps and candles brought the room temperature to a somewhat comfortable level, as long as I was also wearing warm clothing.

This book offers you my experience of what I did throughout many storms and how I prepared for them. When I pulled all my gear together for Hurricane Irma, I thought it would be time to share my preparedness plan with others. As I started to write about my hurricane preparedness, I realized there is much more to consider than just taking shelter during a storm.

I've also learned that after a storm can be even more challenging than the time during a storm. Recognizing how you will weather the storm, preparing to survive and knowing no matter what you are faced with, you will ultimately thrive again.

Hopefully you can take some of these suggestions, apply them to your own life, and make the next storm you encounter an easier ride for all in your home - no matter what the next storm brings your way.

Wishing you safety during any storm ...

Rosemary Augustine

Author's artistic expression of Hurricane Irma.

Hurricane Irma

Hurricane Irma, a Category 4 hurricane, hit the state of Florida on September 10, 2017. The entire state was engulfed in the path of this storm. However, it was the dirty side of the hurricane that made me apprehensive since I live on the Atlantic side of the state. What is the "dirty side" of a hurricane? The "dirty side" is east of the eye wall where the winds are typically stronger and produce tornado activity ... hence, the name "dirty." In the United States, which is in the northern hemisphere, the circulation of a hurricane is counterclockwise. When hurricanes make landfall, the land and its population on the right side of the counterclockwise circulation will encounter more damage from wind and rain and will experience tornado activity and potential storm surge. Not a place you want to be in a hurricane.

Initially, Irma was a Category 4 hurricane that first hit the Florida Keys and later made landfall again on the Gulf Coast of Florida near Naples, as a Category 3, causing severe storm surge, flooding and destruction. As Irma engulfed all of Florida, no place in the state was safe or secure.

There was no place to escape. Evacuation routes were jammed, gasoline and water supplies exhausted, and nerves frazzled several days before the hurricane even hit.

Melbourne, Florida, where I live, was on the dirty side of Irma. In the end, Melbourne got 12 inches of rain and 100+ mph winds from east to west across a 36-hour period. During Irma, a total of 90 tornado sightings were issued in my county alone, and five were in my immediate area. The fear of total destruction that tornadoes cause made me really anxious, especially after the first warning - with me and two cats hovering in my tiny guest bathroom. The cats were real troupers through this. Their animal instincts kicked in. As for me? I needed nerves of steel. Somehow I managed to keep it all together.

My condo complex survived with minimal damage. A few shingles blew off, a couple of fences were lost, and a lot of rain was deposited on the west side of my patio. I lost power for only 14 hours, (I had expected to have no electricity for days). Just across the golf course green, one condo building was destroyed - the patio and screens in shreds, the roof torn off. Just up the street on the corner, a BP gas station was totally demolished.

These signs of destruction showed me how very fortunate I was to encounter this storm in the fortress that I live in. I'm not in a flood zone, but because I live on the 2nd floor, I was concerned about my roof blowing off. I consider myself very lucky and very blessed to have come away unscathed compared to so many others.

However, I believe my preparation had a lot to do with my safety throughout the duration of the hurricane, and importantly, also the type of building I live in here in Florida. A second floor unit in a block construction building, facing north and south was a major consideration when I first bought it in 2015. If I were facing east, I would not have escaped considerable destruction so easily. Those winds off the ocean, all of five miles from me, were vicious, not to mention extremely damaging.

Preparing for the Storm

Hurricane season runs June 1st to November 30th each year. Nor'easters (Mid-Atlantic and New England states) usually occur November to March (and can actually happen just about any time). Snow storms can happen December to April in many areas. When I lived in Colorado, tornado season was in May and June. In California, earthquakes happened anytime. I've lived in a lot of states and encountered all of the above - numerous times.

Now, here in Florida, as Memorial Day approaches, I begin my list of purchasing supplies, and must haves. Some items are already on hand; others need to be replenished because I've used them.

Most importantly, throughout all your preparations, you must be organized. These items and suggestions will help you plan well in advance. It doesn't mean you will enjoy the storm; it only means you will be prepared no matter what happens.

I have listed the things that I find important to have on hand, buying in advance, so that not much has to be bought at the last minute.

I have provided check boxes throughout to help you note what's important to you and your family. Feel free to use colored pens and/or markers to help you highlight what's most significant to you. Use this book as a guide to help you through each storm.

Keep in mind I'm one person with two animals. You may need to adjust some of my suggestions or the amount of food and water to have on hand based on the size of your family, number of children, their ages and of course your pets.

My suggestions also consider being without electricity for at least a week. In some instances you may only be without power for no more than a day or two. Depending on the storm, consider being without electricity for longer periods. With that in mind, you'll cope much better with your supplies and preparations, knowing you can go for a longer period of time without power if necessary.

You may want to converse with neighbors as well, possibly pooling resources, such as grills, shovels, or generators. I'm amazed at how neighbors come together during storms and how many want to help in any way they can. My neighbors have always been a godsend no matter where I've lived.

Just remember, you'll never know the full fury of a storm until you are in it. So preparing for it, and preparing for after it, is most important. If you encounter total devastation, it could be days or weeks before local and federal aid can begin to assist your community.

For Example, when Hurricane Maria hit Puerto Rico, more than 10 days had passed before aid started to reach the island. All of Puerto Rico was without electricity, water, food, and gasoline during that time. And, more than a month later, parts of the island are still without electricity.

All this preparation is really for after the storm, when you are without electricity and with possibly no running water. Being prepared will make the wait for the electricity to be turned back on easier and more comfortable.

Meanwhile, you'll have what's needed to pull through an emergency. However, I can't promise after doing all that I suggest, that the wind won't totally destroy your home and blow away all that you have done to prepare. Let's hope not. A few prayers couldn't hurt in these instances as well.

Water

☐ I'm one person with two cats. I like to have 10 gallons of water on hand including a mix of gallon jugs and 16 oz bottles. Depending on the size of your family, adjust accordingly.

☐ Figure on at least five to seven days without electricity, maybe longer, depending on the destruction. You need water to drink, to cook with, to wash yourself, brush your teeth, etc., and water for your animals.

☐ You may even want to freeze a couple of gallon jugs or 16oz bottles, so when the electricity goes off, those frozen bottles are either in the fridge, the freezer, or available to keep you cool.

I know the plastic bottles are bad for the environment. However, you could possibly encounter a "boil water" order from your city when the lights go out and that would be hard to do with no electricity... unless you have a gas stove.

We encountered a storm a year before Hurricane Irma that knocked out our water treatment plant here in Melbourne, Florida, and although we had electricity, for a week we had to boil water. And, a few weeks after Hurricane Irma, a water main break at the same water treatment plant in Melbourne caused residents to be on a "boil water" alert again, this time for four days. This notice had nothing to do with the hurricane. So sometimes being prepared helps when warnings happen unexpectedly, and they do.

A Few Choice Words

During the days prior to Hurricane Irma hitting the Melbourne area, businesses begin boarding up their windows. As I drove through historic downtown, I saw a few businesses with boarded up windows and all too familiar words spray painted on them:

"Get Lost Irma"

"Matthew 2016 and Irma 2017"

"Hey Irma, take a turn and go out to sea"

"Hey Irma … F#$K Off"

Just a few words I saw that made it both very real what was headed our way, and a few light-hearted quotes that got right to the point.

Gas Stove

☐ Gas stoves are the best when encountering power outages. However, if you don't have one, there are alternatives.

Lucky you if you have a gas stove. With no electricity, even with an electric starter on your gas stove, you can still use it as long as you have matches. Light a match and touch the burner with it while you are turning the knob to light the burner. You can then boil water, cook one-pot meals, heat soup, or make coffee. Although you probably could use your oven in this way, it is not recommended for safety reasons.

No Gas Stove?

☐ Ha! You're in luck. I purchased a one-burner folding stove that uses Sterno (the canned fuel used for chafing dishes at banquets) at Walmart a couple of hurricanes ago. See photo on next page.

☐ Look for this or something like it in the camping section of Walmart, Bass Pro Shops or similar outdoor / camping gear stores. I was able to make coffee for neighbors and cook my lunch right after Irma left us with no electricity.

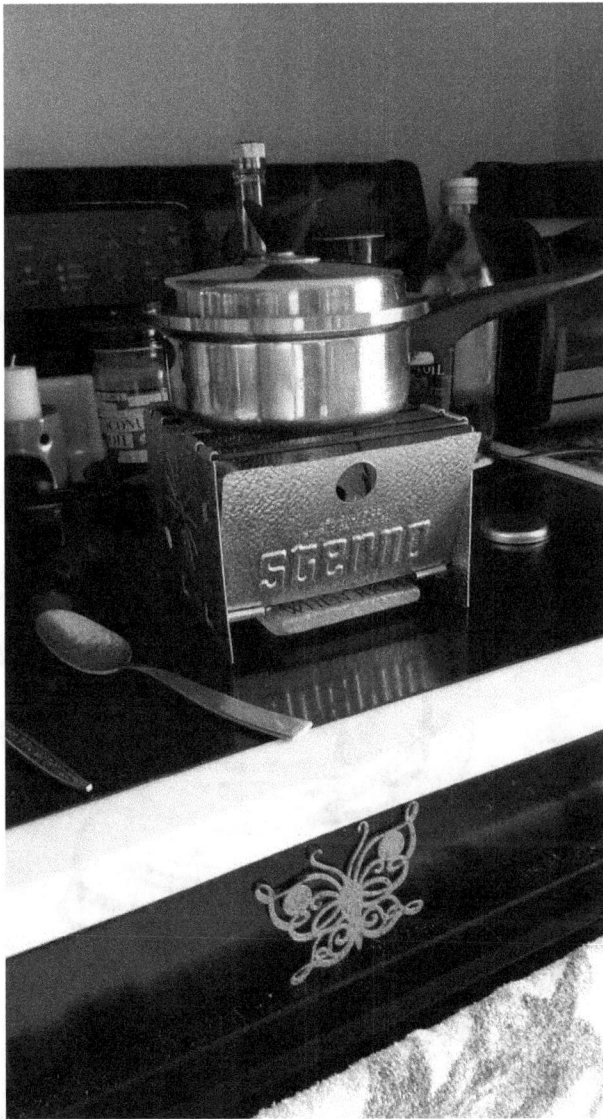

My folding one-burner stove that uses Sterno

Oil Lamp, Candles and Flashlights

This is a preference - oil lamp or candles?

☐ I love candles in jars.

☐ I also have an oil lamp with several bottles of lamp oil.

☐ You can also consider a hurricane lantern.

☐ Remember to also have one or more flashlights with fresh batteries.

For longer power outages, an oil lamp and/or lantern provides better lighting when reading at night than using candles.

In the winter time, I also found that the combination of an oil lamp and candles gave some warmth to the room.

I bought my oil lamp at Walmart in the off season, and when I lived in New Jersey, I bought two at Kmart. I buy the oil to fill it at a local hardware store. Hurricane lanterns are easily found in hardware stores and online.

My pantry just before Hurricane Irma.

Food

I buy non-perishable items, like peanut butter, tuna or other canned fish, soups, beans, crackers, instant coffee, tea, juices, soda, applesauce, granola bars, nuts, etc. For any food you want to prepare using an emergency folding stove or gas stove, look at one-pot meals.

Boxed macaroni and cheese, although not the healthiest of food items, can be a one-pot meal. So can a can of soup, baked beans, tuna sandwich, etc. Snacks, cereals, even pre-packaged polenta, dried fruit, and dried meats, etc., are easy items to use during a power outage.

Shelf stable milk is another item to purchase since it needs no refrigeration and provides the milk and calcium you need throughout the storm, not to mention a welcome drink when eating a peanut butter and jelly sandwich.

Last minute supplies should be purchased a couple of days before the storm is forecast to arrive, items such as bread and cookies from your local grocery store bakery.

The following page begins a list of food items to consider having on hand during a storm.

Food List

☐ Peanut Butter ☐ Jelly

☐ Jerky ☐ Dried Salami ☐ Spam

☐ Tuna ☐ Salmon ☐ Sardines

☐ Soups ☐ Beans ☐ Baked Beans

☐ Bread ☐ Crackers ☐ Dry Cereal

☐ Granola Bars ☐ Cookies

☐ Dried Fruits ☐ Assorted Nuts

☐ Applesauce ☐ Canned Fruit

☐ Shelf-stable milk ☐ Canned milk

☐ Powered milk (uses water)

☐ Canned / bottled sodas:

☐ Seltzer ☐ Club soda ☐ Colas

☐ Various box or canned juices

☐ Other items to have on hand include:

_____ ... _____

_____ ... _____

_____ ... _____

_____ ... _____

_____ ... _____

_____ ... _____

_____ ... _____

_____ ... _____

_____ ... _____

_____ ... _____

_____ ... _____

_____ ... _____

_____ ... _____

_____ ... _____

_____ ... _____

_____ ... _____

_____ ... _____

_____ ... _____

Must Have List

☐ Toilet Paper

☐ Baby Wipes

☐ Candles

☐ Matches

☐ Can Opener and ☐ Bottle Opener

☐ Paper Plates ☐ Paper Bowls ☐ Plastic Cups

☐ Plastic Utensils - necessary unless you want to boil water and do dishes. I didn't think so.

☐ Ziplock bags - Sizes: Quart / Gallon /
        2 Gallon / 2-X and 4-X.

☐ Bleach ☐ Baking Soda ☐ White Vinegar (for clean up afterwards)

☐ Batteries - AA, AAA, C, D, 9 Volt, etc.

☐ Hearing aid batteries

☐ Several different size flashlights with appropriate batteries.

☐ Stock up on BoGo items and 10 for $10 sale items throughout the year, so you have extra of these food items when needed for a storm.

☐ Duct Tape

☐ Plastic sheeting (or heavy duty plastic drop cloths). Even a cheap shower curtain/liner will do in case you suddenly have a window blow out.

☐ Water - gallon jugs and 16 oz bottles.

    ☐ Suggest five to seven gallons per person;

    ☐ Suggest two gallons per pet.

☐ Cash. - Several hundred dollars to a thousand dollars in cash.

    Having watched what happened to Puerto Rico during Hurricane Maria, with up to 10 or more days with no food, water, gasoline or access to ATMs, strengthened my belief to have cash on hand, preferably in small bills during and after a storm.

☐ Does anything else come to mind? Add it here. Keep in mind the following pages will also provide must-haves, or things to consider having on hand.

_____ ··· _____

_____ ··· _____

_____ ··· _____

_____ ··· _____

_____ ··· _____

_____ ··· _____

_____ ··· _____

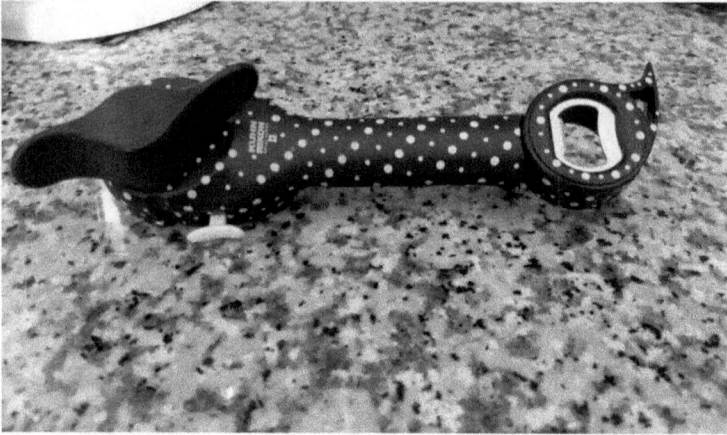

The Best Can Opener...

Opens cans, bottles, pop tops,

and releases seals

Can Opener

☐ A can opener and bottle opener are on the must have list… and here's why:

Although I show a fancy model on the previous page, I love it. Yet, a simple manual version to open cans and/or bottles is all you need for an emergency supply kit.

Remember, some soda bottles that are glass need a bottle opener to remove the cap. And some pop-top cans are difficult to maneuver for older folks, so the one shown handles all that you need. It's more expensive than something you can easily pick up at a dollar store; however, it does the trick in a storm and for every day kitchen cooking.

The version shown on the previous page can be bought at any kitchen supply store. I bought mine at QVC.com. Simpler versions are less expensive and easier to use and can be bought cheaply at dollar stores. Always keep these in your emergency supply kit.

Pet Needs

Animals are smarter than we think. They know what's going on, and their animal instincts kick in during storms. Keep them safe with you, and they'll understand. A little Rescue Remedy goes a long way, since you don't want them too zonked out. Here are some pet items to consider:

☐ Canned / wet food

☐ Fork or spoon to scoop out the canned food

☐ Lid for canned food

☐ Dry kibble

☐ Litter for cats (I also put extra litter and a box in my car trunk just in case we have to evacuate suddenly).

☐ Travel bowls for food and water

☐ Water - preferably a few gallons just for them.

☐ Leash for each animal

☐ Carrier for each animal

Buttercup in her carrier during Hurricane Irma

☐ Rescue Remedy for animals (I'm repeating this because we often forget our animals are stressed too).

☐ Pet's medications, if any

☐ Toys - If you do evacuate, have a couple of toys in their bag as well.

☐ Keep all the pet items together in or with the carrier, as all this goes with you when you take your animal. Even if you stay in your home, have the carriers out and the Rescue Remedy ready. It's about creating comfort for your animals and for yourself

☐ Is there anything else you can think of that you need for your furry friend? Comfort items like a Thunder Shirt; Feliway spray and/or wipes, calming herbs for dogs, etc.

☐ Have your pet's medical records with your important papers that show his/her up-to-date vaccinations and medical history.

☐ Make sure your pet has a tag and/or is micro chipped in case you evacuate and/or head to a shelter.

☐ Have your vet's name, address and phone number in your cell phone. Also have it written on your pet's medical records, if not already listed.

☐ Anything else you want to include to make your pet safe and comfortable during and after a storm?

☐ _____

☐ _____

☐ _____

☐ _____

☐ _____

☐ _____

☐ _____

☐ _____

☐ _____

☐ _____

☐ _____

☐ _____

☐ _____

☐ _____

☐ _____

What to Do
With ALL Those Freezer Items

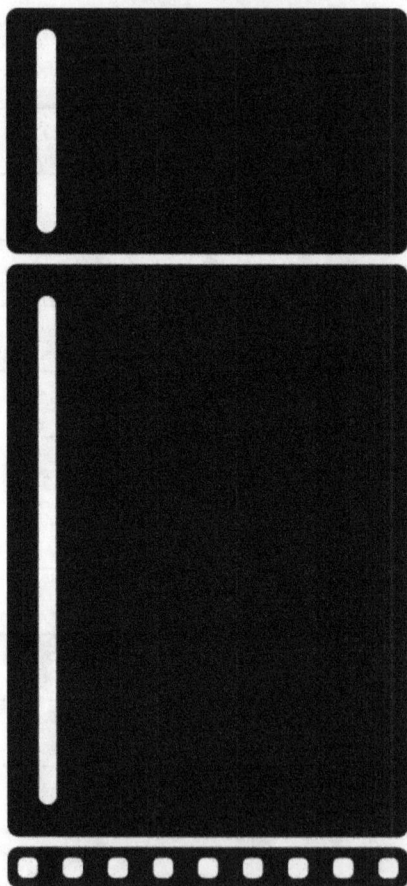

☐ As soon as you know a storm is headed your way, even if it's a week out, start making ice and storing the ice in plastic bags in your freezer. Freeze gallon jugs of water and 16oz bottles as well. These will either keep your freezer cold during a power outage, or move the frozen bottles to the fridge to keep it cold.

☐ Three to five days before the storm is scheduled to reach you, start using up everything in the freezer. Eat it, prepare it, or check the dates and throw it out. This is an option for less waste and making room for gallon jugs of water you may want to put in your freezer to keep everything cold/frozen while the power is off.

☐ Finish off all the ice cream you may have in the freezer, too.

☐ Place a coin on top of a frozen cup of water, or on top of a cube of ice if you use ice cube trays. If the coin is later found at the bottom of the cup or ice cube tray, it will indicate that the items left in the freezer melted and refroze, which means they could be dangerous food items and should not be eaten.

Breakfast quiche before clearing the patio.

Styrofoam Coolers and Quiche

☐ I have two Styrofoam coolers and use them all the time when I go grocery shopping, so my cold and frozen items stay cold / frozen in the Florida heat - just in case I don't go home immediately from the grocery store. However, in anticipation of the power going off, I put a couple bags of ice in the coolers, so the cooler will be cold. Then when the time comes, and we do lose power, I transferred what I want into the coolers by candlelight, and, I add more ice as needed, too.

☐ I love to use these Styrofoam coolers to transfer small items during a power outage like mustard, mayo, remaining milk or cream.

☐ The one thing I don't keep is eggs. But I do make a quiche the day before the storm is due. That way I use up all my eggs, cheese, and frozen veggies when making a quiche. Once it's baked, you can eat it cold or warm while you still have electricity for using the microwave. I ate the quiche before I tore down the patio preparing for Irma. You could also hard boil your remaining eggs as well. These keep well after a storm in your cooler.

Medical Kit

Here are some must-haves for your medical emergency kit:

☐ Peroxide ☐ Rubbing alcohol ☐ Gauze pads

☐ Tape ☐ Band-aids ☐ Ankle /knee wrap

☐ Rescue Remedy for animals (natural calming aid).

☐ Holy Basil for humans (natural calming aid)

☐ Renew prescriptions and just in case you need to evacuate, take all your meds with you, not just a few days' supply.

☐ Vodka ☐ Rum ☐ Whiskey

☐ Beer… ☐ Wine

Drink before the storm as long as you have all your preparations in order. Or drink after the storm. But never, ever drink alcohol during the storm. You will need all your wits about you once the storm hits. Collapse afterwards. Trust me you will.

Batteries and Chargers

☐ Stock up throughout the year on batteries: AA, AAA, C, D, 9 Volt, hearing aid batteries, and any other batteries you may need.

☐ Make sure you have a car charger for your cell phone as well.

☐ If at any time you see a battery operated fan, buy one. You'll use it during warm weather with no air conditioning when the power goes off.

☐ Keep your cell phone, iPad, and other rechargeable items fully charged until the power goes off.

☐ Limit cell phone usage to text only - uses less battery power.

☐ NO live streaming once the lights go out.

☐ Note: You don't know how long you will be without electricity. Figure on at least three days maybe five, longer if your area is really hit hard and parts of your area are destroyed. You could very easily be without electricity for 10 days or more, so being prepared is vital after the storm.

☐ Realize that once your electricity goes out, so does your Internet. Even if you have a satellite dish, you'll probably have a limited Internet connection.

Even cell towers struggle once the electric power goes. You wouldn't think so, but it's because of the draw on the tower usage, while it struggles to work for emergencies.

☐ No electricity also means no ATMs and no use of credit cards to buy gas, food, etc.

☐ Generator …

☐ Gas can …

☐ Gas for the generator

Anything else you want to add to this category?

☐ _____

☐ _____

☐ _____

☐ _____

☐ _____

☐ _____

☐ _____

☐ _____

☐ _____

☐ _____

☐ _____

Games and Toys

Now is a good time to consider games and toys that don't require electricity or that will suck up your fully-charged cell phone or iPad battery. It's time to have a few good games, books, or puzzles to keep you and/or the family occupied.

However, once the storm is over you'll be too busy with assessing damage, cleaning up and using all the supplies I've suggested.

Here are some ideas for games and toys:

☐ A few good board games,

☐ Paperback books,

☐ Travel art supplies - acrylic or water-based paint, brushes, sponge sticks, glue stick, colored pencils, eraser, ruler, paper, journal, or coloring books.

☐ Board puzzles

☐ Cube puzzles

☐ Dice

☐ Jacks

☐ A deck of cards handy for those manual games of solitaire.

Battery Operated Radio

☐ During a storm, you may have the TV tuned to the Weather Channel or better yet to a local channel.

☐ If lightning occurs during the storm, however, it's definitely not advisable to be watching TV.

☐ You certainly want to have a small, battery-operated radio. Set the radio to a local station. Follow the storm, notices, tornado warnings, or other pertinent storm news, especially when the electricity goes out. This will be a lifesaver if more serious conditions develop.

☐ Some may decide to use a crank operated or even solar-powered radio during a storm. I personally prefer a battery-operated one that takes AA batteries.

What's a Bath Tub Doing in a Storm?

Using Your Bathtub

☐ Often overlooked, you can either take cover in the bathtub for tornado warnings (if an interior room) or fill it with water to help flush the toilet when you are without power for days. Your choice.

☐ Take a shower or bath before the storm… and clean the tub before using it for tornado shelter or filling with water for the toilet.

☐ Once the storm starts, be dressed and stay dressed, including wearing non-slip comfortable shoes. Even if the storm continues to rage on throughout the night, sleep in your clothes. You want to be ready to jump and go if necessary. In emergencies, there's no time to start looking for your shoes or changing out of your jammies.

Bags, Bins and Cases

A couple of months before Irma, I had purchased 2-gallon Ziplock bags and 4-X Ziplock bags. I guess I was going to store something in them but never did. When I saw them in the pantry, out they came.

☐ I stored papers in the 2-gallon bags. (These bags measure 13" x 15".)

☐ The 4-X Ziplock bags (measure 2' x 1' 8" and have expandable bottoms) are great for clothes, toys, sports equipment, even electrical equipment like a laptop, computer towers, modems, etc. If you live on the first floor, use these bags for anything you don't want to get wet.

☐ I had put some of these 2-gallon bags filled with documents into a brief case and stored the case in the closet. Since I live on the top floor, I didn't put them on the top shelf, in case the roof blew off.

☐ Do not store documents in the dishwasher as water will enter it if flood waters are more than a foot deep or if the washer becomes submerged.

☐ Suitcases filled with precious items and stowed properly - up high and secure - are a better bet, just not close to the ceiling or attic.

☐ If you live in a two-story home, move as much as you can to the upper floor.

☐ Bins with lids are very helpful too. In my downtown office which is on the ground floor and a block from the Intracoastal Waterway, I pulled all the equipment off the floor and stored all the files from the bottom drawers into the bins. Those bins sat on top of my desk just in case we had water damage on the floor.

☐ I also packed a backpack with two changes of clothing, a towel, cat food, toothbrush and toothpaste, and my personal documents - passport, credit card, cash, and wallet. These were in the plastic bag as well. The backpack gave me the option of free hands if, for some reason, I needed to evacuate suddenly and have to grab two pet carriers.

Well Before the Storm Hits

☐ One thing I did before the storm was even headed my way was to go through my personal documents and updated the following:

☐ My Will

☐ My "In Case of Emergency" paper that I post on the fridge (later stored in a Ziplock bag in the freezer)

☐ I typed up ALL my bank account numbers, credit card numbers with expiration dates, three-digit code, customer service number, etc., and printed off a couple of copies. One copy I keep in my safe.

Although I left my credit cards in my safe as well, I had that list with me, next to my passport. My wallet only had my driver's license, a couple of credit cards, and my medical cards, and of course, cash.

A Few Days Before

☐ Fill your gas tank

☐ Take cash out of the bank and/or ATM. How much? Several hundred dollars or possibly even a thousand dollars if you can. Have small bills such as fives, tens and twenties.

Timing on the above is important, as you can't wait until last minute. With Hurricane Irma, three to four days before the storm hit, there was no gas, no bottled water left in the stores and no cash in the ATMs. Everyone else has the same idea, so think ahead on this one.

Outside the Home

☐ Look at your patios, decks, porches, and lawns. Is there anything that could be moved or picked up and fly through the air even with 50 mph winds? Now think about 100-150 mph winds, with greater gusts and/or the possibility of tornado activity during the storm.

☐ Clear the decks of anything that could be destroyed or become a missile damaging your property or someone else's. This goes for wind chimes, flowerpots, tools, patio furniture, door wreaths, etc. Store safely inside the garage or your home.

☐ Cover the keyholes on your doors so that dust, dirt or other debris doesn't lodge in the keyhole and make the door difficult to lock or unlock.

☐ If you have storm shutters, install and/or close the shutters a day or two before the storm.

☐ Use plywood to cover windows especially for the ground floor, and property facing a wind-prone direction.

☐ Never shim a window so it doesn't rattle. Let it rattle. With the wind and storm energy, the window needs the movement or it will break.

☐ Have sandbags for outside entry ways or flood prone areas around your property. Either pick up the allotted amount when your city is distributing them or make them off-season and store for future use. They can also be easily purchased online - search for sand bags or flood barriers.

☐ Use towels on the bottom of your inside doors, along the bottom of sliding glass doors, and along windowsills, in case doors or windows leak.

☐ What else do you have that could be a missile and/or needs to be secured safely outside your home?

☐ _____

☐ _____

☐ _____

☐ _____

☐ _____

☐ _____

☐ _____

☐ _____

☐ _____

☐ _____

☐ _____

A Note on Supplies

The suggestions in this book are designed to prepare you over time, as it is a lot to do at the last minute. Remember, supplies may not always be available last minute either.

☐ Throughout the year, take advantage of Buy One Get One offers (BoGo) and 10 items for $10 sales.

☐ Check expiration dates. If you don't want to eat all the food you buy for storm supplies, donate after the storm and replenish for the next storm.

☐ You don't need an extra room for all of these supplies. A small space or shelf in your pantry will suffice. Certain items like water, pet food, candles, matches and batteries should always be on hand.

When to Panic

There is no need to panic when you are prepared. The most important part of any storm preparation is preparing so you don't have to panic. When you have supplies on hand and a plan in place - maybe a back up plan as well, you are ready for any storm emergency.

Be prepared and you'll fare far better than you ever expected.

If You Evacuate

Remember, if you evacuate, you still need to bring supplies with you, especially if you go to a shelter. It's a lot of work to have all this on hand and then have to load up a car to leave. However, depending on where you are going, you may or may not have supplies provided to you.

☐ Hence the need to bring food, water, medicine, pet food and supplies and, of course, something to entertain yourself.

☐ If you are going to evacuate to higher ground out of the area, know where you are going and reserve a hotel room far enough in advance. You can always cancel. If you are concerned about cancelation penalties, it just may be worth it. If you wait too long, reservations may be hard to come by.

☐ If you are evacuating due to a hurricane, a new law since Hurricane Katrina requires hotels to accommodate pet owners *and their pets.*

☐ If you are headed to someone else's home that is on higher ground or out of the area, bring all your supplies and animals with you.

☐ If you evacuate to a shelter and you have animals, know in advance the shelters in your area that accept you with your pets.

☐ You may have neither Internet at a shelter nor cell service, but bring your chargers anyway.

☐And, besides all the food, water, and supplies mentioned above, bring your bedding supplies - such as a sleeping bag, pillow, and/or blanket.

After Thoughts

I'm just one person with all these supplies. A family of five certainly increases the need for emergency supplies for each person. Don't let the process be daunting. Let each child participate in the process so they can begin to learn how to be self-sufficient when the need arises for them in adulthood.

If after reviewing this survival guide, you find I've forgotten anything, or there is something that you use and would find helpful for me to share with others, please let me know. My email is listed at the end of this book in my "About the Author" section.

Also realize that all the work you did in preparing for the storm including storing things away, putting up shutters, and clearing the patio, etc., has to be undone. Everything has to be put back, or taken down after the storm.

These storms are a lot of work before and after. Most often there is plenty of time to prepare. However, afterward I'm grateful to have come through with minimal damage, if any. Usually it's only my nerves that get damaged.

Depending on the severity of the storm, realize that afterwards you will feel exhausted. Stress, anxiety, and fear, before and during the storm, take its toll on you and your animals. Be sensitive to this and know that physical and emotional symptoms may appear days or even weeks later after a storm.

Never discount your feelings, and especially pay attention to your pets and their behavior afterwards. Animals are very sensitive to changes in the barometric pressure. Many have different reactions prior, during, and after storms. I found Rescue Remedy to be a lifesaver.

It has been known that both humans and animals can experience Post Traumatic Stress Disorder (a.k.a. PTSD) after a devastating storm, especially a tornado, or a Category 3, 4 or 5 hurricane where total loss and destruction are experienced by a community

Know that you are not alone, and seek help for you or your animal if you find that either of you experience any physical or emotional pain afterwards.

The things I've listed and discussed may not be definitive, but having been in enough storms throughout my lifetime, I have acquired some useful tips and necessities for weathering any storm.

During the storm, I try to pacify myself with distractions, with doing some art, journaling or playing a game. But honestly, it doesn't always work. Mostly I'll watch the trees sway in the fierce winds and cuddle with my kitties. If I've already lost electricity, I'm usually sitting in candlelight and noting my thoughts. Any prayers were said long before the storm arrived.

By the time the storm reaches my doorstep, there is a fascination with the fury and a fear of what might happen running through my veins.

Most importantly, it's time to be flexible. Your life is at stake. No matter how frustrated you may be, never complain about the storm or the conditions afterwards. You're alive and you survived. Maybe this storm wasn't so bad, but the next one could be.

Realize that each storm is different. However, the preparations you put in place ahead of time will pay off in the end, and, just may save your life.

Prayer to Remain Calm

During a Hurricane

When Hurricane Matthew threatened Melbourne, Florida in 2016, I wrote a prayer. Last minute, Matthew went out to sea just south of Melbourne and came back to hit land about an hour north of us. Matthew totally missed us.

I was hoping for the same scenario with Irma. I used this same prayer again, but this time for Irma. Saying it helped me remain calm during a rather harrowing experience.

Find this prayer on the next page.

My Hurricane Prayer

I know there is only one God. A divine presence, a universal being. A God of love and peace. A God that is fearless in times of trouble. A God that is courageous, strong, and resourceful during a hurricane. A universal being that knows the power of calm and relaxation. I know that God is the source of all things, and during this storm, we are one with it. I know that I am an expression of God. I too possess the qualities of love, peace, courage, and strength. I too am fearless, calm, and relaxed. As an expression of God, I understand the storm's fury, and listen to help heal its hurt. Through my understanding of this storm, I am spared, my home is spared, my community is spared. God's home is spared too. I attract only good from the storm and remain fearless throughout. I give thanks with ease and grace knowing my gratitude is what spares me before, during, and after the storm. I release this prayer so that the universe can do its perfect work as I speak. I release any negative thoughts, energy or concerns. And I release any fear surrounding the storm, as I know I am one with God, my divine being. This is the truth, and it is happening right now, because it is so, and so it is. Amen!

About the Author

Rosemary Augustine is an artist and author with over 10 published books. Over the last 30+ years, she has lived in California, Colorado, New Jersey, Pennsylvania and Florida. She has weathered numerous storms during her lifetime including earthquakes, tornadoes, hurricanes, and many winter storms with power outages. Born and raised in Southern New Jersey, her first hurricane was Hazel in 1954. She still has memories of sitting in her parents' kitchen in candlelight and watching a huge tree fall crushing the garage next door.

During one winter storm, Rosemary was featured on ABC Nightly News in February 2014 when she was found shoveling out her car, which was buried in two feet of snow while she was wearing a full-length mink coat. She had no electricity for several days during that storm. Rosemary was 80 miles from the New Jersey coast when Sandy hit in 2012, and she still experienced dangerous storm conditions.

These storms and weather events have molded a sense of preparedness in her. "I've been through more power outages than I can count on both hands, and so flashlights and candles are always close at hand" says Rosemary.

Although Rosemary survived Irma totally unscathed, she again was reminded that her extensive preparations were most important, even more so now living in Florida. Rosemary tweeted throughout the entire storm to chronicle her experience, calm her nerves and to keep her friends around the country informed of her safety. Those tweets can be found at Twitter.com/ZiggysSecrets.

Rosemary has made her home in Melbourne, Florida since 2015. She moved to Melbourne with her famous feline and muse, Ziggy, who is the featured feline in her book *Secrets I Learned From Ordinary House Cats*. When Ziggy died suddenly in the summer of 2016, she continued to find Ziggy her muse, and was spiritually encouraged to continue with her "Ziggy's Secrets" Facebook page and Twitter posts as well as maintaining her website - ThankGodImaFeline.com A few months after Ziggy's passing, Rosemary adopted two six-year old sibling felines - Oscar and Buttercup - who are the new representatives of Ziggy's Secrets online.

The following books authored by Rosemary Augustine can be found on Amazon as well as her websites:

365 Days of Creative Writing

Secrets I Learned From Ordinary House Cats

Ziggy's Secrets

Jenny's Secrets

Adventures with Byron

Journal to a More Creative Self

Bucket List Journal

29 Things to Do

How to Live and Work Your Passion

I Love My Job

Facing Changes in Employment

Find her on the Web at:

RosemaryAugustine.com *and*
ThankGodiMaFeline.com

Social Media includes:

Twitter.com/ZiggysSecrets

Facebook.com/MyCoolCatZiggy
(or use Facebook's search box and enter Ziggy's Secrets)
Pinterest.com/JournalQueen

Linkedin.com/in/RosemaryAugustine

Rosemary can be reached via email:

info@RosemaryAugustine.com

I SURVIVED IRMA

09-10-2017

When our first tornado warning was announced with a blaring siren on my cell phone, the kitties and I headed to our tiny guest bathroom. Buttercup instantly jumped into the sink while Oscar and I sat on the floor. My photo of her was posted on our twitter page and later I turned it into a memes. We will never forget Hurricane Irma.

๙๐ ๙๐